W9-DAD-695

FRANKLIN D. ROOSEVELT

OUR THIRTY-SECOND PRESIDENT

by Melissa Maupin

THE CHILD'S WORLD®

JB
ROOSF

PUBLISHED IN THE UNITED STATES OF AMERICA

THE CHILD'S WORLD®
1980 Lookout Drive • Mankato, MN 56003-1705
800-599-READ • www.childsworld.com

ACKNOWLEDGMENTS
The Child's World®: Mary Berendes, Publishing Director

Creative Spark: Mary McGavic, Project Director; Melissa McDaniel, Editorial
Director; Deborah Goodsite, Photo Research

The Design Lab: Kathleen Petelinsek, Design; Gregory Lindholm, Page Production

Content Adviser: David R. Smith, Adjunct Assistant Professor of History,
University of Michigan–Ann Arbor

PHOTOS
Cover and page 3: White House Historical Association (White House Collection)
(detail); White House Historical Association (White House Collection)

Interior: The Art Archive: 8, 11, 16 and 39 (Culver Pictures), 24 (The Art Archive);
Associated Press Images: 22, 29, 34 and 39; Corbis: 5 and 38, 13, 14, 17, 18, 30
(Bettmann), 6 and 38, 15, 21, 28, 35 (Corbis), 7 (Underwood & Underwood), 10
(Hulton-Deutsch Collection); Courtesy of the Franklin D. Roosevelt Library: 4,
12; Getty Images: 27, 32 (Getty Images), 36 (Popperfoto); The Granger Collection,
New York: 33, 37; The Image Works: 19 (Topham), 25 (Scherl/SV-Bilderdienst);
iStockphoto: 44 (Tim Fan); Jupiter Images: 23 (Ewing Galloway); Library of
Congress: 20 (Dorothea Lange); U.S. Air Force photo: 45.

LIBRARY OF CONGRESS CATALOGING-IN-PUBLICATION DATA
Maupin, Melissa, 1958–
  Franklin D. Roosevelt / by Melissa Maupin.
    p. cm. — (Presidents of the U.S.A.)
  Includes bibliographical references and index.
  ISBN 978-1-60253-060-7 (library bound : alk. paper)
  1. Roosevelt, Franklin D. (Franklin Delano), 1882–1945—Juvenile literature. 2.
Presidents—United States—Biography—Juvenile literature. I. Title. II. Series.

E807.M335 2008
973.917092—dc22
  [B]
                          2008004368

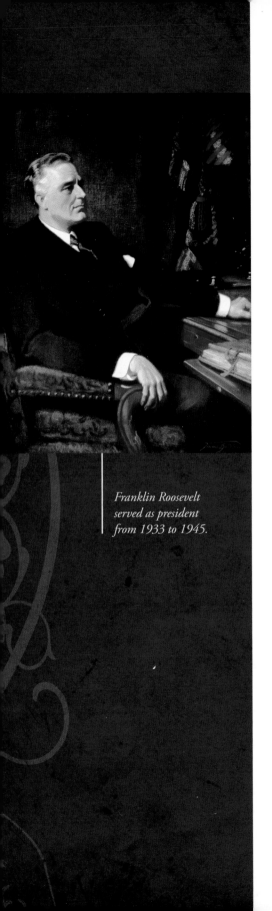

*Franklin Roosevelt
served as president
from 1933 to 1945.*

TABLE OF CONTENTS

CHAPTER ONE

WEALTHY ROOTS

Franklin Delano Roosevelt was a wealthy man who was elected president of the United States at a time when many people were very poor. Roosevelt served as president during the Great **Depression.** This economic downturn cost millions of Americans their jobs. Businesses and banks closed. Many families were homeless and had no money to buy basic items such as food, clothing, or medicine. Roosevelt's goal as president was to fix the problems faced by average Americans. "The test of our progress is not whether we add more to the **abundance** of those who have much," he said. "It is whether we provide enough for those who have too little."

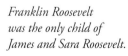

Franklin Roosevelt was the only child of James and Sara Roosevelt.

Although Roosevelt was dedicated to helping poor Americans, he had never been poor himself. In fact, Roosevelt grew up in a wealthy family. His father,

James, was the successful president of a railroad company. He had enough money to supply young Franklin with anything he needed or wanted.

Franklin Roosevelt was born in Hyde Park, New York, on January 30, 1882. He was schooled at his country mansion, as was the custom in wealthy families at the time. His mother, Sara, taught him when he was young. As he grew older, nannies and tutors took over the job of educating him.

As a child, Franklin enjoyed collecting stamps and searching for wildlife in the local woods. Each summer, he could hardly wait to start the family vacation.

Roosevelt grew up in this grand house in Hyde Park overlooking the Hudson River. Roosevelt loved his family home. Late in life, he said, "All that is within me cries out to go back to my home on the Hudson River."

Franklin's mother, Sara Delano Roosevelt, was 26 years younger than her husband. James was a widower and had one son from his first marriage.

Franklin was a big baby and had a difficult birth. He was a bluish color when he was born, and the doctor feared he might not be alive. The doctor blew into Franklin's lungs, and Franklin finally gave a healthy cry. The delivery was so difficult that Sara had no more children after Franklin.

The Roosevelts traveled to Campobello, an island off the Atlantic coast of Canada where they had a summer home. There, Franklin learned to sail and dreamed of working as a sailor one day.

When Franklin was 12, James Roosevelt wanted to send him to boarding school, but Sara refused. She couldn't bear to be without her son. Finally, at age 14, the Roosevelts enrolled Franklin in the Groton School in Massachusetts. He was older than most of the other boys in his classes and had a difficult time making friends. He did meet a boy named Lothrop Brown at Groton. The two boys became best friends and remained close throughout Roosevelt's life.

James Roosevelt, shown here with Franklin, was a businessman, but he preferred spending time in the country. He enjoyed riding horses and fishing.

COUSIN TEDDY

At Groton, Franklin Roosevelt already had a strong interest in politics. One reason for his keen interest was that his distant cousin Theodore (Teddy) Roosevelt was becoming important in the Republican Party. In 1898, Teddy Roosevelt became a hero during the Spanish-American War. In this war, the United States fought to free Cuba from Spanish rule. Roosevelt led a troop of soldiers called the Rough Riders to victory in a battle in Cuba.

In 1900, Theodore Roosevelt was elected vice president. He became president when President William McKinley was killed in 1901. As president, Roosevelt was devoted to trying to improve the lives of average Americans. He called for laws that would protect workers. Franklin was in college by this time. He greatly admired Teddy's energy and desire to improve the nation. He began to think that he, too, might one day enter politics.

After graduating from Groton, Franklin attended Harvard College in Cambridge, Massachusetts. Roosevelt shared his large, elegant apartment with Lothrop Brown. He earned only average grades at Harvard. He spent more energy on his social life than on his studies. But he worked hard to become a reporter for the school newspaper, the *Harvard Crimson*.

After only a few months at Harvard, Franklin received tragic news. His father had suffered a severe heart attack. Franklin finished his classes and then rushed home to be with his family. One month later, James Roosevelt died, with Sara and Franklin at his bedside.

Without James, Sara was alone. To be near her son, she moved to Cambridge. For the rest of her life, Sara lived with or near Franklin.

During his Harvard years, Roosevelt fell in love with his future wife, Eleanor Roosevelt. Eleanor was his fifth cousin. As children, they had played together at family gatherings. Roosevelt hadn't seen Eleanor in several years. On a train trip from Washington to New York, he grew bored and decided to explore the train. In one car, he was surprised to discover the grown-up Eleanor sitting by herself. He sat with her, and they talked for the rest of the trip. After that, they began to date. Roosevelt took Eleanor to dances and parties.

Eleanor may have seemed an odd match for Franklin. Franklin was a dashing young man. He was tall, handsome, and social. He chatted easily with others and enjoyed attending parties and entertaining friends. Eleanor, on the other hand, was considered plain looking. She hated her chin, which she called "weak," and the way her upper teeth stuck out. Eleanor was also quiet and shy. She felt uncomfortable at social events.

When Franklin proposed to Eleanor, his mother was upset. She did not think Eleanor was the right match for her only son. She tried to get Franklin to date other young ladies, but Franklin was not interested. Franklin and Eleanor were married in New York City on March 17, 1905. They went on a tour of Europe for their honeymoon.

After graduating from Harvard, Franklin attended Columbia Law School in New York City. In 1907, he passed the state law exam and began practicing law. He became a law clerk at Carter, Ledyard & Milburn, a New York firm.

As a child, Franklin Roosevelt took many trips to Europe. He also learned how to ride horses, shoot guns, and play polo.

Meanwhile, Franklin and Eleanor had settled into married life. Eleanor gave birth to their first child, Anna, in 1906. Over the following nine years, the Roosevelts had five more children: James, Franklin Jr. (who died as an infant), Elliott, a second Franklin Jr., and John.

Eleanor and Franklin worked to build a happy marriage, but Sara Roosevelt did not make their job easy. She was very close to Franklin and had strong opinions about how he and Eleanor should live. She made household decisions without asking Eleanor's opinion. She also tried to take over the raising of Eleanor and Franklin's children. Sometimes Eleanor fought back, but Franklin rarely supported her. Eleanor often felt alone and frustrated.

Sara Roosevelt did not want her son to marry Eleanor. The two women never became close.

CHAPTER TWO

POLITICS AND WAR

After working at the New York City law firm of Carter, Ledyard & Milburn for a few years, Franklin Roosevelt realized that he didn't like being a lawyer. He wanted to be more of a leader in society. In 1910, **Democrats** asked Roosevelt to run for political office. Franklin found this opportunity exciting. He quit his job and ran for the New York Senate. Roosevelt had money to spend on his **campaign** and boundless energy. He worked tirelessly and won the race.

Franklin Roosevelt in 1913

Once in office, Roosevelt worked to help common people, particularly farmers. He insisted he would not be a friend to the powerful political "bosses" who made many decisions in politics at that time. "I am pledged to no man, no special interest, and to no boss," he said.

Franklin Roosevelt ran for office for the first time in 1910. He enjoyed campaigning, and won election to the New York Senate.

While campaigning for his second **term** in 1911, Roosevelt and Eleanor caught a serious illness called typhoid fever. He was forced to stay in bed for several weeks instead of campaigning. He called a newspaperman named Louis Howe to help him. Howe kept Roosevelt's name in the papers so the voters would remember him. On Election Day, Roosevelt won. Louis Howe would later become one of Roosevelt's political advisers.

The next year, Roosevelt helped Woodrow Wilson campaign for the presidency. Wilson, like Roosevelt, was a member of the Democratic Party, one of the two most powerful **political parties** in the nation. When Wilson won, Roosevelt attended his **inauguration,** where he received a wonderful surprise. Wilson wanted him to be the assistant secretary for the U.S. Navy. Roosevelt had always loved ships and sailing. Now he would be a leader of the largest fleet of ships in the world. He would be able to live in the nation's capital and work with the president.

Roosevelt liked being assistant secretary of the navy. He enjoyed the navy ceremonies and was a strong supporter of increasing the size of the navy.

In 1914, Roosevelt ran for the U.S. Senate. He lost the race, however. He returned to his navy job just as World War I was starting in Europe. The United States wanted no part of the war, but Germany sank an American cruise ship, killing 128 people. Then, in 1917, the Germans announced that they would

Franklin Delano Roosevelt is often referred to by his initials, FDR.

The Roosevelts moved to Albany, the capital city of New York, after Franklin became a senator. Away from Franklin's mother, Eleanor was finally able to take charge of her family. "I had to stand on my own two feet," she remembered, "and I think it was good for me. I wanted to be independent."

Franklin Roosevelt pins a medal on a navy officer. Roosevelt served as assistant secretary of the navy from 1913 to 1920.

James Cox (left) and Franklin Roosevelt campaign together during the 1920 presidential race. Cox, the Democratic presidential candidate, was the governor of Ohio.

bomb any ship that sailed near Great Britain, one of the nations fighting in the war. President Wilson felt he had no choice at this point. He asked Congress to declare war on Germany. World War I was a brutal and bloody fight, but the United States and its **allies** finally won in November 1918.

Following the war, members of the Democratic Party decided they wanted a change in leadership. In 1920, they held their national **convention,** a meeting where they chose their presidential **candidate.** They selected James Cox, who asked that Roosevelt run as the vice presidential candidate. Cox and Roosevelt fought a tough campaign. But in the end, they lost to their Republican opponents, Warren G. Harding and Calvin Coolidge.

With the Republicans in the White House, Roosevelt was out of a job. President Harding selected Republicans as his assistants. Roosevelt left Washington and tried his hand at business, but he quickly grew bored. He dreamed of a thriving political career—in fact, he dreamed of being president. Roosevelt began planning for the future. "The moment of defeat," he told a friend, "is the best time to plan for victory."

Before he could finish his plans, Roosevelt was struck with a staggering challenge. After swimming with his children at Campobello, he became ill. He thought he simply had the flu and went to bed, but his health worsened. His arms and legs ached, and his fever climbed. The next morning, he collapsed as he tried to get out of bed. By that afternoon, his entire body was **paralyzed.**

Franklin Roosevelt spent many happy summers at Campobello Island. He enjoyed canoeing, sailing, and exploring the island's caves.

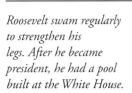

While working to recover from polio, Franklin Roosevelt often exercised in warm water. In 1924, he visited a resort in Georgia called Warm Springs. The hot mineral water that emerged from the ground there seemed to help him. Roosevelt grew to love the resort and spent $200,000 to improve it. He turned it into a treatment center for other polio victims.

Roosevelt swam regularly to strengthen his legs. After he became president, he had a pool built at the White House.

The local doctor said Roosevelt merely had a cold. Eleanor and Franklin's adviser, Louis Howe, believed it was much more serious. The Roosevelts talked to a specialist, who said Franklin had polio, a disease that once crippled many children and some adults. No one knew how to cure polio, and there were few treatments. Roosevelt worried that his political career might be over, but he remained upbeat. He told everyone that he would walk again one day.

Roosevelt worked hard to recover from polio. He exercised daily and especially liked swimming in warm water. Although the paralysis disappeared from most of his body, his legs never fully recovered. He was forced

to walk with braces and crutches or to use a wheelchair. For the first time, Roosevelt knew how it felt to be weak. He felt even more sympathy for people who suffered from poverty, illness, and other troubles.

Roosevelt returned to politics in 1924 by heading Alfred Smith's campaign for president. Giving a speech for Smith at the Democratic National Convention took a great deal of courage for Roosevelt. He had always been strong, and now his legs hardly worked. He wanted to stand on his own to give his speech. Roosevelt brought his son James with him to the convention. James helped his father walk onto the stage, where he stood to speak. The Democrats at the convention felt proud to see Roosevelt working to overcome his disability. The crowded room rewarded him with a round of applause.

Roosevelt read about his election as governor of New York. He served two terms.

After Roosevelt was paralyzed by polio, he was never able to walk without help again. At first, he thought his career in politics was over. His mother wanted him to retire and live a quiet life at Hyde Park. But Eleanor disagreed. She was certain her husband would recover more quickly if he continued to pursue his interests.

In 1928, Alfred Smith, who was governor of New York, asked Roosevelt to run to replace him. Roosevelt didn't agree right away. He was determined to walk again, and he didn't want to stop exercising in warm water. Finally, Roosevelt agreed for the sake of the Democratic Party. Roosevelt did not think he would win the race, but when the votes were in, he was the new governor of New York.

Roosevelt was serving as governor when the **stock market** crashed in October 1929 and the Great Depression began. Before the Depression, many people had invested in the stock market. They had watched their money grow as the market climbed to record heights. Then suddenly, the stock market crashed. Thousands of people lost their fortunes. Businesses failed, and people lost their jobs. With no income, hungry people lined up at soup kitchens for meals. Families lost their homes and were forced to camp in fields using scraps of metal and cardboard boxes as shelters.

Roosevelt set up the Temporary Emergency Relief Administration (TERA) to create jobs for the people of his state. TERA workers improved roads, built parks, and cleaned up buildings. News of Roosevelt's successful program spread across the country. People began to talk of him as a future presidential candidate.

After Roosevelt was elected to a second term as governor, many Democrats wanted him to run for president. Eleanor wasn't sure this was a good idea, but she promised to help him if that was what he wanted to do. "If polio didn't kill him," she once said, "the presidency won't."

During the Great Depression, millions of people had no money for food. Here, men line up for a free meal.

DAILY LIFE DURING THE DEPRESSION

Nearly everyone suffered during the Great Depression. At its worst, 15 million Americans were without jobs. To make ends meet, people did odd jobs, took in ironing, and rented out spare rooms. Many educated and trained workers were forced to sell apples on street corners or shine shoes for change. People begged for jobs. If they couldn't find work, many also begged for money.

"Brother, Can You Spare a Dime?" was a popular song during this time. Most Americans couldn't pay their bills, so many store owners took eggs, butter, cows, and other items in trade. Clothes were used and reused. Mothers passed clothes down to younger children and then used what was left for rags or quilt pieces. Women also made clothes or colorful quilts from cotton feed sacks. People with land had large gardens, and they canned fruits, vegetables, and meats.

During the Depression, some children quit school because they had no shoes or decent clothes to wear. Others traveled with their families in trucks or wagons from town to town, looking for jobs. Teens from large families often left home. They hitchhiked across the country searching for work and food. Many parents felt ashamed that they couldn't support their families. Children did what they could to help. During the Great Depression, many children wrote to President and Mrs. Roosevelt, asking them to help their parents.

CHAPTER THREE

THE NEW DEAL

Franklin Roosevelt saw how sad and desperate the country was. He had ideas about how to help the American people. He grouped these ideas together, calling them the New Deal. Roosevelt wanted to give everyone a second chance. As in a card game, he wanted to deal everyone a new hand, giving them a new chance to succeed.

Roosevelt was first elected president in 1932. Many Americans blamed the other candidate, President Herbert Hoover, for the Depression.

Democrats liked Roosevelt and his ideas. At the 1932 convention, they **nominated** Roosevelt as their presidential candidate. Americans felt hope in Roosevelt's promise of a New Deal. Many believed President Herbert Hoover had done too little to help them since the Depression began. On Election Day, Roosevelt enjoyed a sweeping victory, winning in 42 of the 48 states.

Roosevelt's inauguration day in March 1933 was not the happy celebration that other presidents had enjoyed. He had a challenging job ahead of him. Never had the country's economy been in such desperate trouble. More than a third of American workers did not have jobs. Farmers and ranchers in the Midwest and Great Plains were suffering from a severe **drought.** Many people were homeless. Others were hungry or even starving.

During the 1930s, severe drought hit the Midwest and the Great Plains. As plants withered in the heat, there was nothing to hold the soil in place. Strong winds picked up the soil and carried it away in huge dust storms that blackened the sky. The area became known as the Dust Bowl.

A jobless man sells apples on the street. At the peak of the Great Depression, 15 million Americans were out of work.

Roosevelt knew that he would have to act quickly to turn the country around. He also knew that he needed to calm the fears of the American people. In his inauguration speech, President Roosevelt told the country, "Let me assert my firm belief that the only thing we have to fear is fear itself." Then Roosevelt laid out goals to reopen banks, get people back to work, and offer aid to the neediest Americans. His speech was not just talk. For the next three months, known as "the first hundred days," Roosevelt worked to find solutions. He gathered a wide group of advisers nicknamed the Brain Trust to help him. The Brain Trust included people from many fields, including professors, lawyers, and **economists.**

On February 15, 1933, Roosevelt went to Miami, Florida, to give a speech. When Roosevelt finished his speech, a man pulled a gun and shot at him five times. Although Roosevelt was not hurt, five other people were injured, including the mayor of Chicago, Anton Cermak, who died from his injuries.

Roosevelt shakes hands with supporters. He is the only American president to have been elected more than twice.

Franklin Roosevelt enjoyed collecting stamps, bird watching, and playing cards.

One week after his inauguration, Roosevelt announced the Emergency Banking Bill. The bill called for a bank holiday—a period of time when all banks would close. During this time, the weakest banks with little money would simply close their doors for good. Banks with money would reorganize. These stronger banks could reopen quickly but under new laws that would protect their customers' money.

The new banking laws gave people confidence in banks again. Many people had been hoarding their cash at their homes. Now they felt safe putting money in the bank again. The banks invested the money people put into their accounts. Money began to circulate through the nation's economy again.

One of the major problems the country was facing was the lack of jobs. Roosevelt and his staff created several programs to help employ workers, including the Civilian **Conservation** Corps (CCC), the Civil Works Administration (CWA), and the Works Progress Administration (WPA). The CCC used money from the government to hire young men to work outdoors on public projects, such as clearing land and building dams. The CWA hired men and women to work on other government projects, including building libraries and airports. The WPA hired workers in many different fields. For instance, it hired writers and artists to create guidebooks about the states and art for public places.

The Civilian Conservation Corps (CCC) was part of Roosevelt's New Deal. The CCC hired young men to work on projects such as building roads and improving parks.

President Roosevelt opened the door for minorities and women to serve as high government officials. By 1938, Roosevelt had 20 African Americans serving as advisers. He also appointed Frances Perkins secretary of labor. This made her the first female member of the cabinet, the group of people who advise a president.

To help those living in the worst conditions, Roosevelt pushed through the Federal Emergency Relief Act (FERA). This act set aside $500 million to help the people in the country's neediest cities and counties. Roosevelt also worked to help farmers. Before the Depression, farmers had grown too many crops and could not sell them. Roosevelt set up a system to limit the amount of each crop grown. This way, there would be demand for the crops, and the farmers could sell them for a higher price.

The last two measures of the New Deal came only two years after Roosevelt took office. These measures were the Social Security Act and the Wagner-Connery Act. The Social Security Act set aside money for those who grew too ill or too old to work. The Wagner-Connery Act allowed workers to band together and form **unions.** With unions, workers could fight together for better wages and working conditions.

Some people felt Roosevelt's programs were dangerous. They did not want Americans to depend so heavily on the government. Yet most Americans agreed with Roosevelt's New Deal. In 1936, they eagerly reelected Franklin Roosevelt as president.

During Roosevelt's second term, both he and his wife stayed in touch with the American public. The president regularly had "fireside chats" over the radio to explain how the government was handling various problems. Families gathered around the radio to listen to Roosevelt's calming voice. Meanwhile, Eleanor Roosevelt toured the country, serving as the president's eyes and ears. She listened to the people's problems and thought of ways to help them. She reported back to the president about what she had seen and heard.

As President Roosevelt worked to heal the economy, trouble was brewing in other parts of the world. Germany, Italy, and Japan seemed determined to take over neighboring countries. The United States could stay at a safe distance for a while, but the country's European allies could not. In fact, it wasn't long before nearly all of Europe was involved in World War II. Americans watched the war unfold with horror and fear.

Franklin Roosevelt was the first president to appear on television during his term.

Roosevelt was outgoing. He hosted a cocktail hour each day and enjoyed parties and dinners with friends.

President Roosevelt speaks into four microphones at once during one of his fireside chats.

A NEW KIND OF FIRST LADY

When Franklin Roosevelt became assistant secretary of the navy, the Roosevelts moved to Washington, D.C. Franklin loved their busy life in Washington, but Eleanor did not. A politician's wife was expected to be friendly and enjoy entertaining. Yet Eleanor felt awkward at parties and social events. Often she would stay home.

In 1918, something happened that made Eleanor feel even more insecure. After 13 years of marriage, Eleanor discovered that her husband was having an affair with her secretary, Lucy Mercer. Eleanor was devastated. "All my self-confidence is gone and I am on the edge," she wrote in her journal. Although Franklin worked hard to fix their marriage, it was never quite the same.

Oddly, Roosevelt's affair and his successful career pushed Eleanor to become more independent. Roosevelt's adviser Louis Howe also helped Eleanor gain confidence. He encouraged her to make speeches and travel across the country because Franklin could not.

When she became first lady, Eleanor came into her own. She got involved in serious issues, promoted charities, and made friends with other prominent women. Eleanor joined the League of Women Voters and became a leader in the women's division of the Democratic Party. During her time as first lady, some people called her "Eleanor Everywhere" because she traveled constantly

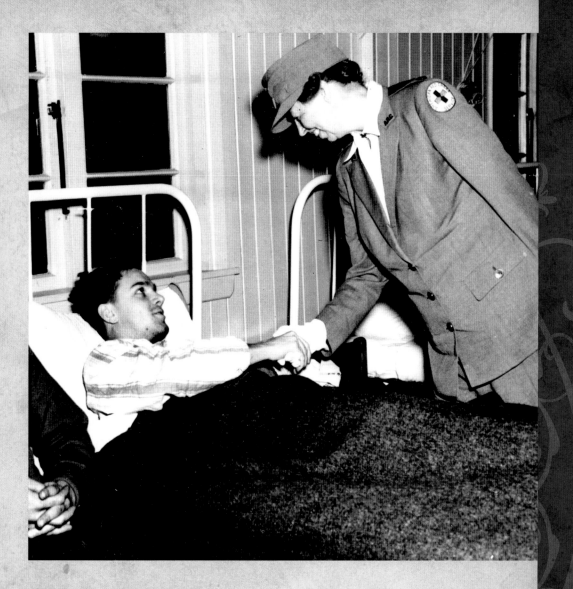

to visit with the American people. Mrs. Roosevelt also wrote books and newspaper columns and gave many lectures.

In 1946, following President Roosevelt's death, she was elected chairperson of the United Nations Human Rights Commission. The goal of the commission was to ensure basic rights for all people around the world. These rights included the right to an education and to free speech. After two years of hard work, the United Nations passed the Universal Declaration of Human Rights, describing these basic rights.

Eleanor Roosevelt died in 1962 at age 78. She was buried next to her husband at their Hyde Park mansion.

FIGHT FOR A FREE WORLD

The Great Depression struck the entire world, not just the United States. Germany in particular faced severe economic problems. In addition to the Depression, Germany owed huge amounts of

President Roosevelt won his third presidential election in 1940. By this time, World War II was raging in Europe, and Roosevelt knew that the United States might need to become involved.

money after losing World War I. The German people were desperate for leadership. They wanted solutions to their problems.

Adolf Hitler stepped in to rule Germany in 1935. Hitler blamed all of Germany's problems on other countries and Jewish people. He also wanted to expand German rule into other countries.

In 1940, Hitler expanded German territory by invading Norway, Denmark, and Belgium. Then Hitler advanced on Holland and France. Winston Churchill was the prime minister of Great Britain at the time. He begged President Roosevelt to send navy ships to help fight the Germans. Roosevelt did not want to get involved in the war, but he knew he had to help. In the end, he loaned Great Britain 50 ships.

During the 1940 campaign for president, the Republican candidate, Wendell Willkie, criticized Roosevelt for helping Britain. He and others feared that Roosevelt was leading the United States into war. After World War I and the Great Depression, most Americans did not want to face another ordeal. Despite such criticism, Roosevelt was easily elected to a third term as president.

The Japanese finally made it clear that the United States would have to fight. Tensions had been rising between the two nations throughout the 1930s. Then, on December 7, 1941, the Japanese bombed the U.S. naval base at Pearl Harbor, Hawaii. This act killed 2,403 Americans and wounded nearly 1,200. The next day, the United States declared war on Japan.

A few months before Winston Churchill became prime minister of Great Britain in 1940, Roosevelt wrote to him. It was a friendly letter of introduction. Churchill wrote back, and the two men quickly became friends. Though they sometimes had different political ideas, their closeness helped both countries through the war.

Japan bombed Pearl Harbor on December 7, 1941. The United States declared war the next day.

In 1940, Franklin Roosevelt became the first person to be elected to a third term as president.

The war changed the United States practically overnight. Young men joined the military. Women stepped in and took the jobs that the men left. Factories geared up to supply the armed forces. Although Roosevelt's New Deal programs had helped ease the pain of the Great Depression, it was the war effort that finally lifted the U.S. economy out of the Depression.

The war was a difficult time for the Roosevelts. Just before Pearl Harbor, Franklin's mother died. In addition, they were concerned for their four sons, who had enlisted in the armed forces. Still, the Roosevelts never wavered. In the president's fireside chats, he assured the people that the government was doing everything possible to win the war. Mrs. Roosevelt knitted sweaters and socks for U.S. troops and traveled overseas to visit wounded soldiers.

After Japan bombed Pearl Harbor, some Americans feared that Japanese Americans might be more loyal to Japan than to the United States. In 1942, Roosevelt issued an order that allowed the military to round up people of Japanese descent. More than 110,000 Japanese Americans—two-thirds of them born in the United States—were moved to guarded camps. Most stayed in these camps until the end of the war.

During World War II, Great Britain, the **Soviet Union,** and the United States were known as the Allies. The main goal of the Allies was to take back the countries of Europe. Gradually, the German army weakened as it battled Soviet forces in the east.

In 1988, the United States government apologized to Japanese Americans for their treatment during the war.

During World War II, three million American women worked in war plants. This woman is building an airplane.

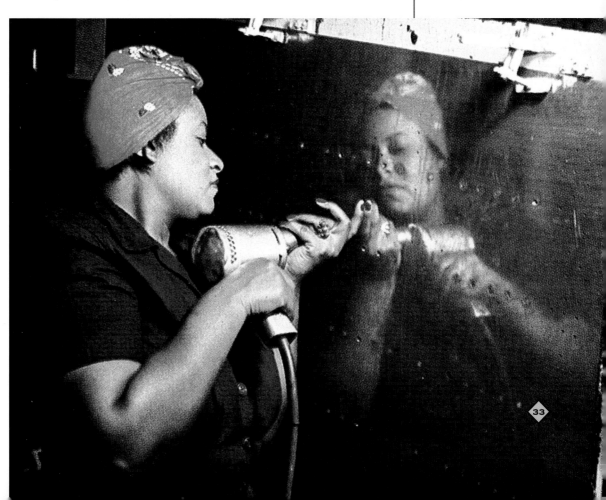

Meanwhile, Roosevelt and Churchill helped plan the Allied invasion of Europe, code-named "D-Day." On D-Day, June 6, 1944, Allied forces splashed ashore on a beach in the French region of Normandy. After heavy fighting, the Allies won the battle. They were able to drive the Germans out of France over the next few months.

American troops also won huge victories against the Japanese in the Pacific. Yet the war raged on. By the presidential election in 1944, Roosevelt was exhausted. He accepted his party's nomination, but he did not feel it was right to campaign. "In these days of tragic sorrow, I do not consider it fitting," he said. That year, Harry Truman was chosen as his vice-presidential candidate.

President Roosevelt and British prime minister Winston Churchill became close friends during World War II.

Roosevelt won a fourth term as president and continued his work to win World War II. Roosevelt met with Churchill and Joseph Stalin, the leader of the Soviet Union, in February 1945 at the Yalta Conference in what is now Ukraine. The "Big Three," as they were called, felt certain that an Allied victory was right around the corner. They made plans for the end of the war. Roosevelt returned from his meeting very tired. For the first time, he addressed Congress in his wheelchair instead of standing with his crutches.

Roosevelt was the only person to be elected president four times. No one else will ever be able to match this record. In 1951, the 22nd **Amendment** was added to the U.S. **Constitution**. It states, "No person shall be elected to the office of president more than twice."

Franklin Delano Roosevelt did not live to see the final victory of the Allies in World War II. On April 12, 1945, he died in Warm Springs, Georgia, of a massive brain **hemorrhage.** It was just 25 days before Germany **surrendered,** ending the war in Europe. Roosevelt's death deeply saddened Americans. For 12 trying years, they had counted on his steady guidance. Just before his death, Roosevelt was working on a speech. "The only limits to our realization of tomorrow will be our doubts of today," he wrote. "Let us move forward with strong, active faith."

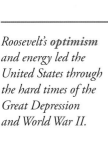

*Roosevelt's **optimism** and energy led the United States through the hard times of the Great Depression and World War II.*

THE ATOMIC AGE

In August 1939, scientist Albert Einstein sent a letter to President
Roosevelt warning him about a new danger. By splitting the center
of atoms, Einstein said, it was possible to make a devastating
weapon called the atomic bomb. He warned the president of
the danger if Germany or another hostile nation built an atomic
bomb first. Roosevelt listened.

In 1942, the U.S. government began the top-secret Manhattan
Project to develop an atomic bomb. In 1945, the government tested
the first atomic bomb at a site in New Mexico. Throughout the war,
the United States and Great Britain believed that German scientists
were working on a similar weapon.

After Roosevelt's death, Vice President Harry Truman became
president. The war in Europe ended in May 1945, but the war in
Asia continued, with great loss of American lives.

President Truman made a difficult decision. He decided to
use atomic weapons to end the war. He warned the Japanese
that if they did not surrender, their nation would suffer complete
destruction. But the Japanese did not give up.

On August 6 and 9, 1945, the United States dropped atomic
bombs on the Japanese cities of Hiroshima and Nagasaki. More
than 100,000 people died in the explosions, and many more
suffered severe injuries. On August 14, Japan finally surrendered—
eight days after the first bomb was dropped. The photo above
shows Hiroshima after the bomb exploded.

TIME LINE

1882
On January 30, Franklin Delano Roosevelt (FDR) is born in Hyde Park, New York, to James and Sara Roosevelt.

1896
FDR enters the Groton School in Massachusetts.

1900
FDR enters Harvard College in Cambridge, Massachusetts.

1903
On June 24, FDR graduates from Harvard.

1904
FDR enters Columbia Law School. His fifth cousin, Theodore Roosevelt, wins the presidential election in November.

1905
On March 17, Franklin Roosevelt marries Eleanor Roosevelt.

1907
FDR passes the New York State law exam. He begins working as a law clerk at the firm of Carter, Ledyard & Milburn in New York City.

1910
FDR is elected to the New York Senate.

1913
President Woodrow Wilson appoints FDR assistant secretary for the U.S. Navy.

1914
FDR is defeated in an election for the U.S. Senate. World War I begins in Europe.

1917
The United States enters World War I.

1918
World War I ends.

1920
FDR runs as the Democratic candidate for vice president. James Cox is the Democratic presidential candidate. Republicans Warren G. Harding and Calvin Coolidge defeat Cox and Roosevelt.

1921
Roosevelt contracts polio after swimming at Campobello in August.

1924
FDR reenters politics as manager of Alfred Smith's presidential campaign. Smith loses the race.

1927
FDR founds the Georgia Warm Springs Foundation, a therapy center for the treatment of polio victims.

1928
FDR is elected governor of New York.

1929
The stock market crashes, and the Great Depression begins.

1930
FDR is reelected governor.

1932
FDR is elected president.

1933
FDR survives an assassination attempt in Florida. On March 4, he is inaugurated as the 32nd president. During the first 100 days of his presidency, Roosevelt presents a wide variety of projects to help end the Depression. His plans are known as the New Deal.

1935
FDR signs the Social Security Act and the Wagner-Connery Act, which allows workers to form labor unions.

1936
FDR is reelected president.

1939
World War II begins in Europe.

1940
FDR sends ships to help Great Britain fight Germany. In November, FDR wins a third presidential election.

1941
On December 7, Japan bombs Pearl Harbor, Hawaii. The United States declares war on Japan. As commander in chief of the armed forces, FDR helps plan major offensives in the war.

1942
The U.S. government rounds up more than 110,000 Japanese Americans and holds them in camps.

1944
Allied troops invade Europe on D-Day, June 6. By the end of the summer, the Allies successfully drive Germany out of France. FDR is reelected president on November 7. He is the only American president to be elected four times.

1945
In February, FDR attends the Yalta Conference with Winston Churchill and Joseph Stalin. The three leaders discuss what will happen at the end of the war. On April 12, Franklin Roosevelt dies in Warm Springs, Georgia. He is buried in Hyde Park, New York. Vice President Harry Truman becomes president. Germany surrenders 25 days after FDR's death, ending the war in Europe. The United States drops atomic bombs on Japan in August. Japan surrenders, and World War II ends.

1962
On November 7, Eleanor Roosevelt dies.

GLOSSARY

abundance (uh-BUN-dunts) If you have an abundance of something, you have a lot of it. Roosevelt did not want to add abundance to those who were already wealthy.

allies (AL-lyze) Allies are nations that have agreed to help each other by fighting together against a common enemy. In World War II, the Soviet Union and Great Britain were allies of the United States.

amendment (uh-MEND-munt) An amendment is a change or addition made to the U.S. Constitution or another document. The 22nd Amendment states that no president can be elected to more than two terms.

atoms (AT-umz) Atoms are the smallest possible pieces of an element (such as silver or lead). By splitting atoms of an element called uranium, experts can make an atomic bomb.

campaign (kam-PAYN) A campaign is the process of running for an election, including such activities as giving speeches or attending rallies. Roosevelt campaigned across New York to become a state senator.

candidate (KAN-duh-det) A candidate is a person running in an election. The Democrats chose Roosevelt as their vice presidential candidate in 1920.

conservation (kahn-sur-VAY-shun) Conservation is the protection or careful management of something. The Civilian Conservation Corps helped protect and improve parks.

constitution (kon-stih-TOO-shun) A constitution is the set of basic principles that govern a state, country, or society. The 22nd Amendment to the U.S. Constitution was approved in 1951.

convention (kun-VEN-shun) A convention is a meeting. The Democratic and Republican political parties hold national conventions every four years to choose their presidential candidates.

Democrats (DEM-uh-krats) Democrats are people who belong to the Democratic political party. Democrats asked Roosevelt to run for office.

depression (dih-PREH-shun) A depression is a period of time in which there is little business activity and many people are out of work. The Great Depression began in 1929.

drought (DROWT) A drought is a long time with little or no rain. During the 1930s, the Great Plains suffered from a severe drought.

economists (ee-KON-uh-mists) Economists are people who study the making, selling, and use of goods and services. Roosevelt asked economists to help him find ways to end the Depression.

hemorrhage (HEM-er-rij) A hemorrhage is uncontrollable bleeding in part of the body. Roosevelt died of a severe brain hemorrhage in 1945.

inauguration (ih-naw-gyuh-RAY-shun)
An inauguration is the ceremony that takes place when a new president begins a term. Roosevelt attended President Wilson's inauguration.

minorities (my-NOR-ut-eez) Minorities are people who are different in some way from other members of a group. Roosevelt paved the way for having minorities serve in high-level government jobs.

nominated (NOM-ih-nay-ted) If a political party nominated someone, it chose him or her to run for a political office. In 1932, the Democrats nominated Franklin Roosevelt as their presidential candidate.

optimism (OP-tuh-miz-um) Optimism is the habit of expecting everything to turn out for the best. Roosevelt had great optimism.

paralyzed (PAYR-uh-lyzd) If someone is paralyzed, he or she cannot move parts of the body. Roosevelt was paralyzed by polio.

political parties (puh-LIT-ih-kul PAR-teez) Political parties are groups of people who share similar ideas about how to run a government. Roosevelt belonged to the Democratic political party.

politics (PAWL-uh-tiks) Politics refers to the actions and practices of the government. Roosevelt had a strong interest in politics as a young boy.

Republican Party (re-PUB-lih-ken PAR-tee) The Republican Party is one of the two major political parties in the United States. Theodore Roosevelt, Franklin's cousin, was a member of the Republican Party.

Soviet Union (SOH-vee-et YOON-yun) The Soviet Union was a country that stretched from eastern Europe across Asia. It broke apart into several smaller countries in 1991.

stock market (STOK MAR-kit) The stock market is where people buy and sell pieces of ownership in different companies, called "shares" or "stock." After the stock market crash of 1929, millions of Americans lost their businesses and jobs.

surrendered (suh-REN-durd) If an army surrendered, it gave up to its enemy. Germany surrendered just 25 days after Roosevelt's death.

term (TERM) A term is the length of time a politician can keep his or her position by law. A U.S. president's term is four years.

unions (YOON-yunz) Unions are groups of workers who join together to accomplish a goal. The Wagner-Connery Act allowed workers to form unions.

THE UNITED STATES GOVERNMENT

The United States government is divided into three equal branches: the executive, the legislative, and the judicial. This division helps prevent abuses of power because each branch has to answer to the other two. No one branch can become too powerful.

EXECUTIVE BRANCH

PRESIDENT
VICE PRESIDENT
DEPARTMENTS

The job of the executive branch is to enforce the laws. It is headed by the president, who serves as the spokesperson for the United States around the world. The president signs bills into law and appoints important officials such as federal judges. He or she is also the commander in chief of the U.S. military. The president is assisted by the vice president, who takes over if the president dies or cannot carry out the duties of the office.

The executive branch also includes various departments, each focused on a specific topic. They include the Defense Department, the Justice Department, and the Agriculture Department. The department heads, along with other officials such as the vice president, serve as the president's closest advisers, called the cabinet.

LEGISLATIVE BRANCH

CONGRESS
*Senate and
House of Representatives*

The job of the legislative branch is to make the laws. It consists of Congress, which is divided into two parts: the Senate and the House of Representatives. The Senate has 100 members, and the House of Representatives has 435 members. Each state has two senators. The number of representatives a state has varies depending on the state's population.

Besides making laws, Congress also passes budgets and enacts taxes. In addition, it is responsible for declaring war, maintaining the military, and regulating trade with other countries.

JUDICIAL BRANCH

SUPREME COURT
COURTS OF APPEALS
DISTRICT COURTS

The job of the judicial branch is to interpret the laws. It consists of the nation's federal courts. Trials are held in district courts. During trials, judges must decide what laws mean and how they apply. Courts of appeals review the decisions made in district courts.

The nation's highest court is the Supreme Court. If someone disagrees with a court of appeals ruling, he or she can ask the Supreme Court to review it. The Supreme Court may refuse. The Supreme Court makes sure that decisions and laws do not violate the Constitution.

CHOOSING
THE PRESIDENT

It may seem odd, but American voters don't elect the president directly. Instead, the president is chosen using what is called the Electoral College.

Each state gets as many votes in the Electoral College as its combined total of senators and representatives in Congress. For example, Iowa has two senators and five representatives, so it gets seven electoral votes. Although the District of Columbia does not have any voting members in Congress, it gets three electoral votes. Usually, the candidate who wins the most votes in any given state receives all of that state's electoral votes.

To become president, a candidate must get more than half of the Electoral College votes. There are a total of 538 votes in the Electoral College, so a candidate needs 270 votes to win. If nobody receives 270 Electoral College votes, the House of Representatives chooses the president.

With the Electoral College system, the person who receives the most votes nationwide does not always receive the most electoral votes. This happened most recently in 2000, when Al Gore received half a million more national votes than George W. Bush. Bush became president because he had more Electoral College votes.

THE WHITE HOUSE

The White House is the official home of the president of the United States. It is located at 1600 Pennsylvania Avenue NW in Washington, D.C. In 1792, a contest was held to select the architect who would design the president's home. James Hoban won. Construction took eight years.

The first president, George Washington, never lived in the White House. The second president, John Adams, moved into the house in 1800, though the inside was not yet complete. During the War of 1812, British soldiers burned down much of the White House. It was rebuilt several years later.

The White House was changed through the years. Porches were added, and President Theodore Roosevelt added the West Wing. President William Taft changed the shape of the presidential office, making it into the famous Oval Office. While Harry Truman was president, the old house was discovered to be structurally weak. All the walls were reinforced with steel, and the rooms were rebuilt.

Today, the White House has 132 rooms (including 35 bathrooms), 28 fireplaces, and 3 elevators. It takes 570 gallons of paint to cover the outside of the six-story building. The White House provides the president with many ways to relax. It includes a putting green, a jogging track, a swimming pool, a tennis court, and beautifully landscaped gardens. The White House also has a movie theater, a billiard room, and a one-lane bowling alley.

PRESIDENTIAL PERKS

The job of president of the United States is challenging. It is probably one of the most stressful jobs in the world. Because of this, presidents are paid well, though not nearly as well as the leaders of large corporations. In 2007, the president earned $400,000 a year. Presidents also receive extra benefits that make the demanding job a little more appealing.

★ **Camp David:** In the 1940s, President Franklin D. Roosevelt chose this heavily wooded spot in the mountains of Maryland to be the presidential retreat, where presidents can relax. Even though it is a retreat, world business is conducted there. Most famously, President Jimmy Carter met with Middle Eastern leaders at Camp David in 1978. The result was a peace agreement between Israel and Egypt.

★ *Air Force One*: The president flies on a jet called *Air Force One*. It is a Boeing 747-200B that has been modified to meet the president's needs.

Air Force One is the size of a large home. It is equipped with a dining room, sleeping quarters, a conference room, and office space. It also has two kitchens that can provide food for up to 50 people.

★ **The Secret Service:** While not the most glamorous of the president's perks, the Secret Service is one of the most important. The Secret Service is a group of highly trained agents who protect the president and the president's family.

★ **The Presidential State Car:** The presidential limousine is a stretch Cadillac DTS.

It has been armored to protect the president in case of attack. Inside the plush car are a foldaway desk, an entertainment center, and a communications console.

★ **The Food:** The White House has five chefs who will make any food the president wants. The White House also has an extensive wine collection.

★ **Retirement:** A former president receives a pension, or retirement pay, of just under $180,000 a year. Former presidents also receive Secret Service protection for the rest of their lives.

F A C T S

QUALIFICATIONS

To run for president, a candidate must

* ★ be at least 35 years old
* ★ be a citizen who was born in the United States
* ★ have lived in the United States for 14 years

TERM OF OFFICE

A president's term of office is four years.
No president can stay in office for more than two terms.

ELECTION DATE

The presidential election takes place every four years on the first Tuesday of November.

INAUGURATION DATE

Presidents are inaugurated on January 20.

OATH OF OFFICE

I do solemnly swear I will faithfully execute the office of the President of the United States and will to the best of my ability preserve, protect, and defend the Constitution of the United States.

WRITE A LETTER TO THE PRESIDENT

One of the best things about being a U.S. citizen is that Americans get to participate in their government. They can speak out if they feel government leaders aren't doing their jobs. They can also praise leaders who are going the extra mile. Do you have something you'd like the president to do? Should the president worry more about the environment and encourage people to recycle? Should the government spend more money on our schools? You can write a letter to the president to say how you feel!

1600 Pennsylvania Avenue
Washington, D.C. 20500
You can even send an e-mail to: president@whitehouse.gov

BOOKS

Feinstein, Stephen. *The 1930s from the Great Depression to the Wizard of Oz*. Berkeley Heights, NJ: Enslow Publishers, 2006.

Lange, Brenda. *The Stock Market Crash of 1929: The End of Prosperity*. Philadelphia: Chelsea House, 2007.

Oshinsky, David M. *Polio: An American Story*. New York: Oxford University Press, 2005.

St. George, Judith. *Make Your Mark, Franklin Roosevelt*. New York: Philomel Books, 2007.

Senker, Cath. *How Did It Happen? World War II*. Farmington, MI: Lucent Books, 2005.

Thompson, Gare. *Who Was Eleanor Roosevelt?* New York: Grosset & Dunlap, 2004.

VIDEOS

FDR: A Presidency Revealed. DVD (New York: A&E Home Video, 2005).

The History Channel Presents The Presidents. DVD (New York: A&E Home Video, 2005).

National Geographic's Inside the White House. DVD (Washington, DC: National Geographic Video, 2003).

INTERNET SITES

Visit our Web page for lots of links about
Franklin D. Roosevelt and other U.S. presidents:

http://www.childsworld.com/links

Note to Parents, Teachers, and Librarians: We routinely verify our Web links to make sure they are safe, active sites—so encourage your readers to check them out!

INDEX